LEEDS The Back to front Inside out, Upside down city

PATRICK NUTTGENS

STILE BOOKS 1979

Contents

Front cover pictures are (from the top) the Black Prince in City Square, Town Hall, Victoria Hall soon after its opening, Kirkstall Abbey, River Aire at Leeds Bridge.
Pictures on page three, (left to right, top to bottom) Potternewton Court, Corn Exchange, Queen Square, Kirkstall Abbey, St John's Church, City Markets.

Changing Face of Leeds.

First published in 1979
by Stile Publications
Mercury House, Otley.

Printed in Great Britian
by Chippendale Press, Otley.

Photosetting by
Eagle Graphics, Ilkley.

I.S.B.N. 0 906886 00 7

Acknowledgements

The basis of this book was a BBC television documentary by Dr Patrick Nuttgens, who thanks the following for their invaluable assistance with the photographs or the text: Leeds City Libraries, Yorkshire Post, Keith Gibson, Leeds City Council Department of Planning, John Edenbrow, Gordon Wilcock, Ann Fairburn, Judith Helman, Eric Sigsworth, Maurice Beresford, Bridget Nuttgens and the BBC, especially Frank Mills and his colleagues.

Kirkstall Abbey

A Place on the River

The first and most constant problem with the City of Leeds is to find it. There never was a more faceless city or a more deceptive one. It hasn't a face because it has too many faces, all of them different; it's a city without logical unity.

To visitors coming by rail from the south, it can be a dreary carpet of red-brick crowded houses, crushed by roads and viaducts, with chimney pots reaching up nearly to the level of the railroad, every year more derelict or brushed away under a new carpet of empty land and motorways. To others, especially those coming in from the north, it is the home of culture and learning – famous for its music and for its university, one of the largest and most prestigious in the country. To others it is nothing more nor less than the Town Hall, the most instantly captivating and memorable of all the great town halls of the Victorian era, the very symbol of the Industrial North.

What it is not, except to those who are looking hard for its history, is its river. Where, after all, *is* the river? It's not very obvious: most of the time not even visible; certainly not yet exploited as one of the assets of the city. (People in Leeds often don't even know it is there). And yet the river is the reason for Leeds' existence and lies at the very heart of the city. Rivers usually do. As Gibbon remarked in *The Decline and Fall of the Roman Empire.* "The servitude of rivers is the noblest and most important victory which man has obtained over the licentiousness of nature".

Not that the River Aire is especially licentious or heroic in its character. It flows down from the Pennines as steady and determined as the city on its banks. It is the middle one of three rivers, roughly parallel to each other. The Wharfe runs down through Ilkley: the Aire through Keighley, Bingley and Leeds: the Calder joins the Aire and all at length enter the Humber and the sea.

Leeds straddles the Aire at the crucial place where the foothills come down to the plain, where the routeways are controllable, where the water could be used and where everything was at hand. The streams or rivers that give Leeds its shape are the Hol Beck, the river Aire, the Sheepscar Beck and the Wike Beck. Where they join together is Leeds, across it the main roads from north to south (Ripon to Wakefield) and north east to south west

(York to Chester).

There was a settlement here, part of the little British kingdom of Elmete after the departure of the Romans, and the Parish Church probably has origins in the eighth century, when Leeds is first heard of – in Bede's *History of the English Church and People.* It was then called *Loidis,* an obscure name probably deriving from an early name for the turbulent river. But the oldest parts of the Leeds which you can walk through today date from after the Norman Conquest and the devastation when William the Conqueror, enraged by two rebellions in the north, marched up to York, destroyed it and then methodically carried out the "harrying of the north" in the winter of 1069 to 1070.

The new feudal settlement which grew up after that devastation was a scatter of villages and manors later enclosed within the city. Such a village was Adel, with its 12th century church, elaborately carved porch and ominous bronze door handle. But the most dramatic relic is the Abbey of Kirkstall on the banks of the River Aire, about three miles up-river from the middle of the city.

It was founded by Cistercian monks, members of an exceedingly austere Order, the keenest and most rigorous colonisers of their day. They looked for sites of wilderness and difficulty, and brought to them sophisticated skills in agriculture and industry. Yorkshire, remote, hilly and cold, and largely undeveloped since the Norman Conquest, might have been created for them. One group founded the Abbey of Rievaulx in 1131. Another settled at Fountains Abbey in 1132, in what was described as a place fit for the dens of wild

Kirkstall Abbey, a surprising relic of the past to find in a built-up suburb of Leeds.

beasts. Fountains grew so quickly that in 1147 thirteen monks set off from it to found a daughter house. They had been given a site at Barnoldswick, up in the Craven hills, but found it unsuitable and moved down to Airedale. Here in 1152 they built a new Abbey – known first as the Abbey of Headingley, soon after as the Abbey of Kirkstall.

It is a solid testimonial to the Cistercians' rejection of elaboration and display. The main building works were complete by about 1175 – very like Fountains, a church with a choir and nave and aisles and transepts and a tower that was at first low (as a Cistercian tower should be) and only later heightened, again like Fountains, just before the Reformation. The monastic buildings were grouped round the cloister, dating essentially from the same period as the church, related to a developed system of water supply and drainage. The whole complex was built of millstone grit, tough and formidable – and lending to the ruins, conceived as a demonstration of austere simplicity, a grandeur unimagined at the time.

Although there are no contemporary accounts of Kirkstall that give an idea of what life was like, the report made at the time of what Aelred found at Rievaulx in the twelfth century gives a daunting picture of Cistercian abbey life in its early years:

> *"......they were clothed in undyed wool spun and woven from the pure fleece of the sheep ...... They venerate poverty, not the penury of the idle and negligent, but the poverty directed by a necessity of the will and sustained by the thoroughness of faith and approved by divine love.*
>
> *"They are welded together by such firm bonds of charity that their society is as terrible as an army with banners...... Counting riches and honours as dung ......spurning the fleshly desires and vain glory in food, drink...... they observe at all times a discreet uniformity using only so much and such means of sustaining life as will just maintain the needs of the body and their fervour in the worship of God. For them everything is fixed by weight, measure and number. A pound of bread, a pint of drink, two dishes of cabbage and beans. If they sup, the remnants of their former meal are dished up again except that instead of the two cooked dishes, fresh vegetables, if they are to be had, are served. When they rest on their beds, each of them lies alone and girdled in habit and tunic, in winter and summer. They have no personal property; they do not even talk together."*

In the ruins of this massive home of an industrious community, you can still picture the activity and effect of the place in its surrounding countryside. The monks of Kirkstall originated many (if not most) of the activities that were to transform a collection of scattered homesteads into a major city. For here was everything they needed – water, hills, minerals, clay and (underneath the ground) coal. The monks exploited them all; they were farmers, foresters, tanners, coal-miners, iron-smelters, coppersmiths, potters and – most definitive of all – spinners and weavers. And that was the industry that made Leeds what it is today.

There could not have been a place more strategically sited. As the forests were cleared and the slopes of the hills used for grazing sheep, wool production became possible on an unprecedented scale in the valleys and hills of the West Riding. There was plenty of grass and plenty of water. The clothmakers worked at home, in workshops attached to their houses, in families or in groups. It is a landscape that has not changed much since the end of the Middle Ages.

As the clothing industry developed, the weavers brought their cloth to town – for dressing and cropping and dyeing – and for marketing – by merchants who became the richest and most influential citizens.

The centre of that town was originally a cluster of buildings down the river from Kirkstall, near the parish church of St Peter. None of that mediaeval parish church survives; because in 1841 it was replaced by the present church, a somewhat gloomy and portentous edifice, stuffed with galleries and monuments that emphasise the seriousness of religion. The original church, built (it was said) *"like a cathedral structure"*, lay in a *"fruitful and enclosed vale"*. From it Kirkgate, the road leading to the church, scrambled upwards to the west. But what became in the 13th century the centre of the town was not Kirkgate, but a road forming the spine of a new town founded at the river crossing a few hundred yards upstream in 1207 by the Lord of the Manor, Maurice Paynel. The road was Briggate, the road leading to the bridge.

That single piece of planning was absolutely fundamental. Briggate was a street wide enough to hold a market. On either side of it were about thirty plots of land reaching back in long narrow strips; on those plots were built the houses and workshops; on them later were grouped the yards and buildings as they became more and more crowded and overbuilt.

To the west led Swinegate and Boar Lane. On that side lay the manor. And there also, at a bend and fall in the river, lay the mills for grinding corn, fed by a lead or goit taken across to them, where the railway station is today.

The population in the 14th century, before the Black Death, was about 1,000 for the whole parish, of whom about 400 lived in the new town. In the 15th and 16th centuries it began to grow rapidly. The weavers brought their cloth for finishing into the town. There were tenters for stretching and drying cloth, dye-vats, a fulling-mill, a coal-mine and a forge. Wealth increased – and so did the population. By the 16th century it was more than 3,000 and quickly doubled again.

There must have been a bridge at the foot of Briggate from early times, although there is no mention of one before the 14th century. There was certainly a fine stone bridge there at the end of the Middle Ages with a chantry chapel on it, like the one at Wakefield. (The present cast iron bridge was built in 1873). The market was at first held on or near the bridge. But it was the moving of the market up into Briggate itself which gave Leeds much of its character and led to the erection of some of its major buildings.

It happened in the 17th century. After the Civil War,

The old Moot Hall in Briggate

Old Leeds Bridge in Lower Briggate photographed in 1867. The Bridge, which dates back to the 14th century had a chantry chapel built upon it and the Cloth Market was held there in the 16th and 17th centuries.

when the town was captured by the Parliamentarians in 1643, and a disastrous outbreak of plague in 1645, when birds flying over the town were said to have dropped dead in the streets, trade revived on an even larger scale than before. Again the population grew – to about 9,000 by the end of the 17th century and over 10,000 in the 18th. And such was the pressure on space in the cloth market at Leeds Bridge that in 1684 it was moved up into Briggate.

The food and provisions market took place at the top of Briggate by the market cross in a space contained by the Moot Hall or Guildhall built by the Corporation in an unusual effusion of civic pride in 1711. It had great Corinthian pilasters at the end and a big statue of Queen Anne which was erected amid great rejoicing in 1713 and is now housed, with a new nose and chin, in the City Art Gallery. From there down to the river was the cloth market. And that market is the scene of one of the most famous descriptions of historic Leeds – Daniel Defoe's account of the market in his *Tour through the Whole Island of Great Britain* of 1724.

> *"The clothiers come early in the morning with their cloth; and as few clothiers bring more than one piece, the market being so frequent, they go into the inns and publick-houses with it, and there set it down.*
>
> *"At seven o'clock in the morning..... the market bell rings; it would surprise a stranger to see how in a few minutes, without hurry or noise, and not the least disorder, the whole market is fill'd; all the boards upon the tressels are covered with cloth, close to one another as the pieces can lie long ways by one another. And behind every piece of cloth, the clothier standing to sell it.*
>
> *"As soon as the bell has done ringing, the merchants and factors, and buyers of all sorts, come down and coming along the spaces between the rows of boards, they walk up the rows, and down as their occasions direct. Some of them have their foreign letters of orders, with patterns seal'd on them, in rows, in their hands; and with those they match colours, holding them to the cloths to their colours, or that suit their occasions, they reach over to their clothier and whisper, and in the fewest words imaginable the price is stated; one asks, the other bids; and 'tis agree, or not agree, in a moment.*
>
> *"The merchants and buyers generally walk down and up twice on each side of the rows, and in little more than an hour all the business is done; in less than half an hour you will perceive the cloths begin to move off, the clothier taking it up upon his shoulder to carry it to the merchant's house; and by half an hour after eight o'clock the market bell rings again; immediately the buyers disappear, the cloth is all sold, or if here and there a piece happens not to be bought, 'tis carried back into the inn, and, in a quarter of an hour, there is not a piece of cloth to be seen in the market.*
>
> *"Thus, you see, ten or twenty thousand pounds value in cloth, and sometimes much more, bought and sold in little more than an hour, and the laws of the market the most strictly observed as ever I saw done in any market in England; for,*

1 Before the market bell rings, no man shows a piece of cloth, nor can the clothiers sell any but in the open market.

2 After the market bell rings again, nobody stays a moment in the market, but carries his cloth back if it is not sold.

3 And that which is most admirable is, 'tis all managed with the most profound silence, and you cannot hear a word spoken in the whole market, I mean, by the persons buying and selling; 'tis all done in a whisper.

"By nine o'clock the boards are taken down, the tressels are removed, and the streets cleared, so that you see no market or goods any more than if there had been nothing to do; and this is done twice a week. By this quick return the clothiers are constantly supplied with money, their workmen are duly paid and a prodigious sum circulated thro' the country every week".

Ultimately however, business people prefer to go indoors and in any case it is more efficient. Worried by competition from a new cloth hall in Wakefield which threatened to draw away trade from Leeds market, the merchants and traders of Leeds built a *"stately hall for white cloths"* in Kirkgate in 1711 – a two storey hall around a quadrangle with pillars and arches and a gilded cupola. It was replaced in 1775 by a new White Cloth Hall, of which just the facade remains, a battered remnant of the busy place in which there were 1,213 separate stalls at which clothiers from the West Riding exhibited their products and sold them to merchants, who then had the pieces dyed and finished and distributed. At the other end of the town, the Coloured Cloth Hall was built in 1758 roughly where the Post Office now stands.

The commerce was prodigious. The number of pieces of broad cloth produced in the West Riding increased from 30,000 to 300,000 in a hundred years; narrow cloths from 60,000 to 130,000 pieces. And most of it passed through Leeds.

Adel church porch.

St John's Church, Briggate

Brief Elegance

Inevitably the town expanded and was distinguished by new buildings. Already in the 17th century, new churches had begun to express the changes and variations in religious practice, especially the popularity of Non-conformism.

Reflecting the Puritan influence which the Parish Church did not satisfy, St John's Church was built at the top of Briggate in 1634. Perpendicular on the outside like a survivor of the Middle Ages, it was richly furnished inside with elaborately carved pews and screens and pulpit and a hefty roof structure with carved angels and musicians and decorations in every available space. It is one of the few really original bulidings in Leeds.

Forty years later a Presbyterian chapel was built on Mill Hill, and twenty years after that meeting places for Quakers and Congregationalists. Boar Lane on the other hand had been changing into the West End of Leeds and a fashionable residential area. To designs by William Halfpenny the church of Holy Trinity was built in 1726. The tower was blown down by the wind early in the 19th century and the present tower was built in 1841.

Holy Trinity Church which was built in 1726 punctuates a Boar Lane which is rapidly undergoing modernisation. The present tower was erected in 1841.

The Assembly Rooms well after their heyday

By that time another dignified chapel, the Brunswick Methodist Chapel, had been built in 1825, with a magnificent interior and organ.

All of that reflected the fact that from the late 17th century, through the 18th century and into the beginnings of the 19th century, Leeds was rapidly becoming, not only one of the busiest and most prosperous urban centres in the north of England, but also a town of some elegance and distinction. You may have to search for the signs nowadays, but they are certainly there.

What happened? If you look at Cossins *New and Exact Plan of the Town of Leeds* of 1725, you can see at once the shape of the town, the compactness of its streets, the gardens everywhere – garths with tenter frames, crofts, ley lands, parks, bowling greens and ings or meadows: and both punctuating the map and lining its margins drawings of the churches and merchants' houses in the new style with Georgian grace.

If you then look at Giles' *Plan of Leeds* of 1815 you can see how the town had spread a little in a hundred years; but more significantly, how it had reshaped itself inside the old boundaries. There are the new Cloth Halls, the new Infirmary behind the Coloured Cloth Hall, more buildings around the river. The main street is crammed with inns and shops and houses. The strips of land behind have become congested and built up, forming tight little yards with houses and warehouses and workshops. One of them had a large house, a counting-house, packing shops, a stable and coach-house, a dunghill, a garden and a close in an area no more than 30 yards wide and 120 yards deep. A few only

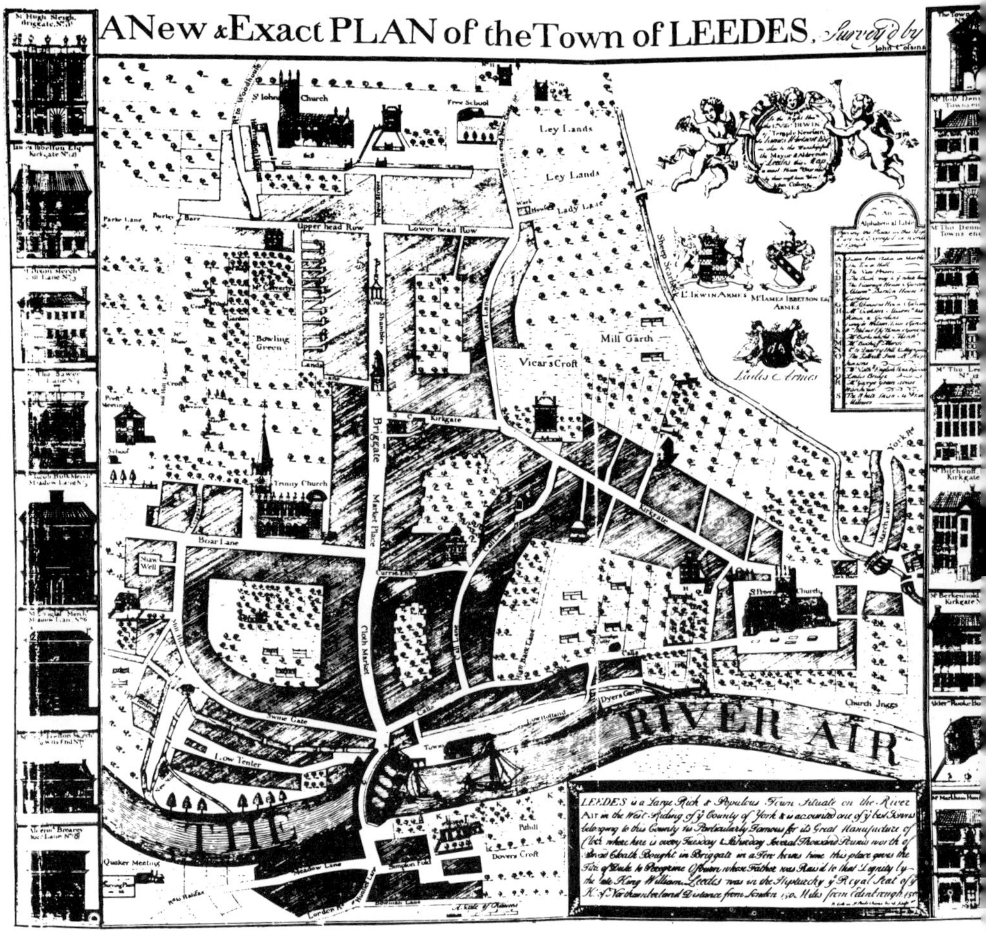

The small, compact town of Leeds in the early 18th century is vividly conveyed in Cossin's New and Exact Plan of the Town of Leeds, published in 1725.

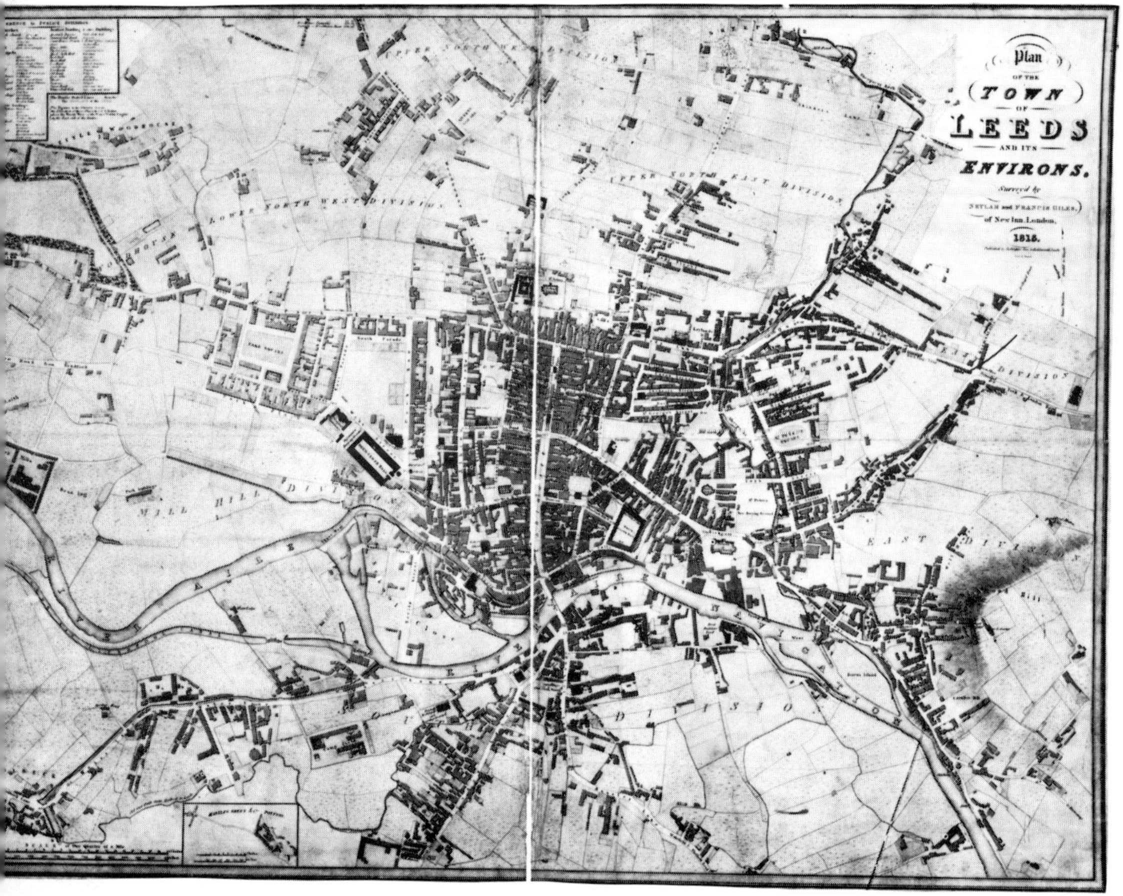

Giles Plan of Leeds of 1815 shows the tight but growing cluster of buildings to the north of the Aire. The square on the left just above centre is Park Square.

A typical view of the old Leeds. This is Rose and Crown Yard, Briggate, pictured in 1887. It was demolished to make way for Queen's Arcade. A few similar yards survive, even today.

Queen Square whose elegant Georgian terraces were built in the early 19th century.

survive in parts of central Leeds but are disappearing rapidly in the face of new developments for which their grouping and size and hemmed-in shapes are unsuited (still nevertheless some of the most evocative and rewarding explorations that you can make today).

But what the map also shows vividly is the beginning of new kinds of building – the movement of the town outwards (though not very far out) into new terraces and squares. The new Assembly Rooms were built in 1775 beside the White Cloth Hall, a truly symbolic juxtaposition of trade and social life that remains typical of the city. It is still there, also sadly in decline as a building but proudly showing its big Palladian window.

The new residential districts were laid out, as in many other towns, to the west and north, the more wealthy moving away from places that they themselves had overbuilt, from the smoke and smell of the finishing shops and the streets which a visitor in 1768 described as "exceedingly dirty, ill-built and badly paved".

Of the new districts the most complete was that to the west of the Coloured Cloth Hall and the Infirmary, on the remaining land of the parks. By 1780 a few houses had been built in Park Row and South Parade. In the 1780's the new streets took shape; East Parade was begun in 1785 and the whole area formed a huge uneven rectangle with the Infirmary and the Coloured Cloth

Hall along the south.

In 1788 Park Place and Park Square were begun. Now the houses are mainly occupied as offices; but Park Square still retains its elegance, and the gardens in the centre, thick with trees, frame the red-brick houses. They were very good houses and *very* expensive. They were occupied by merchants, clergy, lawyers and surgeons; at one time in the late 18th century virtually all the mayors and aldermen for several years lived either in the Square or in one of the Parades or Streets beside it. It was after all the age of elegance.

Further extensions took place to the northwest and north. Hanover Square was laid out in the 1820's, making a setting for the noble Denison Hall of 1786, a three-storeyed pedimented palace housing one of the richest of the merchant families. Near it Woodhouse Square was built in the 1830's, this time a little below the handsome 18th century Claremont, now the headquarters of three of the learned and amenity societies. To the north of the town centre Queen Square was an irregular group of pleasant late Georgian houses; from 1831 onwards a long terrace, Blenheim Terrace, reached up the road towards Woodhouse Moor.

But by the time these estates were built, the richer merchants and industrialists had already begun to move still further out and set up as country gentlemen reasonably close to their work, in rural areas which have now been enclosed by the modern city.

Of the mansions which now survive within its boundaries, the greatest, now owned by the City and forming a major part of its museum, was Temple Newsam, the earliest parts built in the early 16th century, added to and transformed into the house that there is today, in the 1630's. It is of brick with stone dressings and forms three sides of a court. Round the top in huge stone letters the owner made his declaration:

Denison Hall built in Hanover Square in 1786 was one of the palatial mansions occupied by the gentry.

> *"All Glory and Praise be given to God the Father the Son and the Holy Ghost on High Peace on Earth Good Will towards Men Honour and True Allegiance to our Gracious King Loving Affection amongst his Subjects Health and Plenty be within this House".*

It was a happy declaration and probably worth while in view of the fact that a previous owner a hundred years before had been executed by Henry VIII.

That was Lord Darcy, who was involved in the tragic Pilgrimage of Grace of 1536. Henry gave the house to the Earl of Lennox whose son Lord Darnley married

Temple Newsam, the elegant 17th century stately home on the eastern borders of the city. Above the declaration of loyalty in stone and right, the magnificent carved oak staircase.

Mary Queen of Scots. It was Arthur Ingram, who bought the house in 1622, who commissioned and partly designed the major reconstruction that formed the present house. To it was added Garrett's stable block in the 1740's and such famous interior features as C.E. Kempe's great oak staircase in Elizabethan style in 1894. Capability Brown made his usual contribution by transforming the landscape in the 1760's. With the death of the last descendant of the Ingrams in 1871 the house passed to his widow, daughter of the Earl of Halifax. Leeds Corporation bought it in 1922 and made it into a public park and a most evocative gallery and museum.

But Temple Newsam was not really typical of the mansions of the Leeds merchants; it was the home of a great landed family. More typical was the smaller Weetwood Hall of 1625, with sash-windows inserted in the 18th century and later additions in the 19th century, a traditional Yorkshire manor house separate from the city, of the kind bought by the merchants. That is now used as a residence for students of the University of Leeds.

More characteristic still were the new houses and the parks of the richer merchants. Gledhow Hall is attributed to the architect John Carr of York and is dated 1767 though much of it looks later. Meanwood Hall, now part of the Meanwood Park Hospital, was designed by John Clark about 1830. The same architect was responsible for the handsome Mansion in Roundhay Park. The estate had been sold by Lord Stourton in 1797; the purchasers, a London banker and a Leeds banker and merchant, divided it up and began to develop it. The mansion was erected about 1820. It was the greatest of the late Georgian mansions in Leeds and looks it still today, with its giant portico of four columns and a huge pediment. But what makes Roundhay so spectacular is its park, now a public park. The two lakes were created in 1815, the larger one appropriately named the Waterloo Lake. And north of it, constructed a few years later, is a sham castle, a typical folly of the time.

Meantime, to the west of the city on the south bank of

Roundhay Park's Waterloo Lake

Roundhay Park Mansion House

the river, the industrialist Benjamin Gott had purchased the manor of Armley for use as a leisure spot. Then he decided to live there and commissioned Sir Robert Smirke, the architect of the British Museum, to design a new house. Gott's mansion, its wings now removed, is still there in what has been renamed Gott's Park. It was in its time as fashionable as could be, in a rather stern neo-Grecian style. The park itself was laid out by Humphrey Repton, the most eminent and imaginative landscape designer of his time.

From the top of Gott's Park, it is just possible still to imagine the elegance and harmony of Georgian Leeds. It is an appropriate place to do so, and appropriate too to look over the river towards the north at the great sprawling city which Gott himself did not see. He had made for himself an estate in keeping with his wealth and a retreat from the grime of the city, a landscape fresh and unimpaired by obtruding buildings. He might well enjoy it. For he more than any other man was responsible for changing the face of Leeds, creating its new fortunes but destroying in it for ever the very grace and harmony which he tried to recapture in his park.

Rotunda, Roundhay Park.

Middleton Colliery Railway

Gathering Industry

In 1792 Gott established his new factory at Bean Ings, on the north bank of the river Aire, west of the city centre. He had been an apprentice since 1780 in the firm of woollen merchants, Wormald and Fountaine. He took them over in 1790. But the founding of the factory at Bean Ings meant more than another chapter in the life of a successful merchant. It was the start of the factory system for the woollen industry. And it meant that the geography of the town was turned back to front.

It was a drastic reversal of the classic pattern of residential dwellings in the west. For the factory belched smoke and the prevailing wind carried it into the drawing rooms of the elegant houses of Park Square. In 1827 the owner of the land sold all his remaining property south and west of Park Square; what filled it was low cost, high density housing for the workers in the factory and the other mills which were filling the remaining spaces – dyehouses, warehouses, scribbling-mills and fulling-mills, some of them taking over the good brick houses of Park Lane and South Parade. Court cases were taken out repeatedly in an attempt to stop the smoke. Gott was prosecuted for smoke nuisance in 1824. To no effect. Leeds was off to another start and nothing was going to stop it. The population, which had been just over 16,000 in 1770 and had grown steadily to 30,000 in 1800, took off and more than doubled during the next thirty years. By then the out-townships began to be counted along with the population of the borough, making 50,000 in all. By 1841 Leeds was a town of over 150,000 people. In 50 years it had been almost wholly transformed.

Why had Gott placed his factory in such an anti-social place? Simply because, as a man of clear perception and common sense, he could see that it was a key location, not so much for water power as for communications which had developed significantly in the preceding hundred years.

In 1699 an Act of Parliament was passed to make the Aire and the Calder navigable – and to link them, and thus Leeds and Wakefield, with the Ouse, the Humber and the sea. The Aire and Calder Navigation made Leeds, situated at its western extremity, an inland port. Not only therefore could it gather to its markets cloth and goods from the hills of the West Riding; it had as an outlet for its goods, produced by the factory system, routes to almost every part of the country. Via the Aire, the Ouse and the Humber it could reach the Trent navigation, the canals of the Midlands, London and the south.

Then, in 1770, was authorised the construction of the canal from Leeds to Liverpool. It was not completed until 1816. But even before it was completed, Leeds had become, no longer a terminus, but a strategically important junction for the crossing of the North of England. Gott's mill was planted close to the end of the canal in Leeds, where, after coming down through innumerable locks from the Pennines, it stops beside the Aire at the canal dock and warehouse and links to the Aire and Calder Navigation through a simple lock.

The river had come into its own again. And not only the river. In the 1740's and 50's a new network of turnpikes completed connections which were not already there by water. Turnpikes were built to Halifax and Elland, to Bradford, to Selby, to Otley and Skipton, to Harrogate and Ripon, to Wakefield, Barnsley and Sheffield, to Tadcaster and York, and thus to the Great North Road, to north and to south.

In the midst of such a network of communications Leeds was a natural place for manufacture of many kinds as well as wool textiles. It became an important tanning centre and the major linen manufacturing centre, supplied by flax grown east of the city. And there were other important developments.

In the 1790's a penniless mechanic walked into Leeds and begged a night's lodging. His name was Matthew Murray and within a few years he had established himself as a prolific inventor and a founder of the engineering industry in Leeds. He was responsible for the machinery for flax spinning which made the factory system productive. He invented machine tools, steam engines, and his own ingenious system of gear wheels to change the straight line motion of pistons into rotary motion. In 1812 he built the locomotives for Blenkinsop's rack-railway that plied up and down the slopes between Leeds and Middleton Colliery, claimed to be the first railway in the world. He also, in his own house in Leeds,

Bean Ing Mills, the earliest factory proper in Leeds

The Leeds-Liverpool Canal played a vital role in the development of Leeds. Forgotten by most of the citizens, the canal is still going strong.

created the first centrally heated building in the world, colloquially known as Steam Hall.

Murray's memorial, an obelisk of cast iron, stands lonely and ignored in what was once a graveyard and is now an untidy piece of open space beside high flats. Like Gott, he was responsible for many of the changes that transformed the city in the early years of the 19th century. None of these changes was more important than the exploitation of coal to the south of the river. The waggon way from the colliery ran down to the Aire in the middle of Leeds and the town had an ample supply of coal at very advantageous prices. And that in turn encouraged the growth of industries which thrived on coal – chemical works, potteries, glassworks, brick-works and iron foundries, as well as the ubiquitous works for cloth dyeing.

Under a canopy of smoke which lasted for over a hundred years, the town grew and filled almost every vacant space. The river came into its own again, and Leeds became an inland port. Warehouses and factories lined the river and crowded round the old centre. Ships and barges plied along it. And the water still supplied, not only transport, but power to the mills. It was all to change again; but for the moment Leeds was still the place on the banks of the River Aire, where, as Dyer recorded in his poem *The Fleece,*

> "........ *tumbling waters turn enormous wheels,*
> *Where hammers, rising and descending, learn*
> *To imitate the industry of man".*

The Old Leeds Parish Church

Landscape of Chimneys

The coincidence in the heart of industrial Leeds of the river, the navigation and the canal needed only one further addition to bring all the modes of transport together.

Leeds was not in the vanguard of railway mania; that was a privilege claimed by York. But when it did come it came with force. The first railway after the famous Middleton Colliery railway was the line to Selby, opened in 1834; the train set off with 150 passengers and covered 4½ miles in two hours. The first stations lay east and west at the ends of the main industrial and residential districts – at Marsh Lane, from which the line took off to Selby, and then at Wellington Street in 1848.

The railways added to the total recasting of the waterside that the early years of industrial change in the 19th century had brought about. Take for example the bridges. Wellington Bridge was built in 1817 and widened in 1873. Wellington Street itself, straight and unsmiling, was a product of that rebuilding. Down Aire Street, Monk Bridge was built in 1827 and renewed in 1886. In the centre of the town Victoria Bridge, carrying Neville Street, was built in 1839. Crown Point Bridge, further east near the Parish Church, was built in 1842; and still further east South Accommodation Road Bridge was built in 1829 and replaced in 1889.

But the most drastic change of all was bringing the railways into the very centre beside the river. First came Central Station, opened in 1854 on Wellington Street. Then in 1865 permission was given to extend the North East line from Marsh Lane into the middle of the city. It reached there in 1869 and terminated in City Station. Unpretentious in itself, it rests on wonderful dramatic arches over the terminus of the canal and the bend in the River Aire, the most picturesque and macabre of all the scenes in Leeds.

In practical terms, much more macabre was what it did on its way there. Not only did its brick arches cut right through areas of housing, forming great sheds under the arches and cutting off what little view the residents might have briefly enjoyed; they and the embankments also wiped away, in the most totalitarian manner, two of the most prestigious and important buildings in Leeds. The railway sliced through the White Cloth Hall, leaving only a piece of facade. The clothiers and merchants had to move to a new hall in King Street in 1868, a site now occupied by the Metropole Hotel. With that curious flat realism that Leeds business people seem to have, they just shifted along; noting, no doubt equally realistically, that since the development of the factory system, the Cloth Hall was not doing such good business as it used to.

What was still more extraordinary was that the railway also sliced right through the parish churchyard. As part of the deal the railway company undertook to remove the gravestones and put them back as nearly as possible vertically above the right graves. What they did instead was to line the slopes of the embankment near the church. They had some over. The stones are still there over a hundred years later, waiting to be re-erected.

The bravado and coolness with which this environmental tragedy was perpetrated, isolating the Parish Church from the centre of the town and utterly destroying its surroundings, was the uncompromising statement of an industrial giant which knew where it was going and had the self confidence of success. Brougham, speaking in the Cloth Hall in 1830 declared "We don't now live in the days of barons, thank God; we live in the days of Leeds, of Bradford, of Halifax and of Huddersfield". He might have added the names of many other towns in the growing complex of the West Riding, all rivals and independent of each other, which were transforming it into an endless conurbation of darkness and industrial grime.

Leeds itself had already changed. By the middle of the century its engineering industry had taken over as the biggest employer from textiles; then in the 70's it was to develop as the main centre of ready-made clothing. The population rose from 50,000 in 1800 to nearly 500,000 a hundred years later. And the town spread. In that same century its area increased from two square miles to 29 square miles.

A landscape of chimneys provoked the wonder and sometimes the detestation of visitors. Dickens described it in 1847 as the "beastliest place, one of the nastiest I know". He hadn't looked far enough. For among the beastliness were some of the wonders of their time.

John Marshall, having inherited a modest fortune, devoted it to the spinning of flax by machinery. Marshall's Mill was designed by Ignatius Bonomi in Egyptian style and built between 1838 and 1840 at a time when that style, made popular by Napoleon's campaigns, was fashionable and adventurous. It has battered walls, papyrus and lotus flower capitals and is said to have been based on the temple at Edfu. But it was not just the architectural style that was revolutionary. It was a revolutionary concept of the organisation of the building and its function.

Whereas the great mills of the 18th century had been multi-storey buildings, of brick and timber or cast iron, with the constant danger of fire because of the need for heat in the manufacturing process, Marshall's Mill took the problem a logical step further and was built on one floor, spread across a huge space. The interior, of which engravings made in the 1840's show it at work, was constructed of iron columns and shallow brick vaults. In the centre of each vault is a roof light designed to give even illumination over the whole floor. There are 66 glass domes. Looked at outside they are quite surrealist.

Designed like an Egyptian Temple by Ignatius Bonomi, Marshall's Mill is a remarkable example of the exotic whims of the Victorians.

But what must have been even more surrealist was the flock of sheep which, it is said, grazed on the grass covered roof, whose earth and planting kept the workroom warm below.

Marshall's Mill is the most famous of the industrial buildings in Leeds. Its chimney was a version of Cleopatra's Needle. More noticeable, especially to those entering the city by train, was the chimney of the Tower Works, constructed as a red-brick copy of Giotto's marble campanile at Florence Cathedral – an ingenious disguise for a dust extraction plant.

Much the most entrancing and romantic of the industrial buildings, however, was St Paul's House, in the once elegant Park Square, built in 1878. It is a warehouse, now restored, recast and converted for office use, in Moorish style, carried out in terracotta, with many-centered arches, arcades and exotic decoration. Its owner was John Barran, the founder of the modern clothing industry – the pioneer of mass-produced ready-made clothing. As Mayor he contributed to the buying of Roundhay Park for the public; the circular temple at the top of the hill constructed as a drinking fountain records his generosity and his success.

Roofscape of Marshall's Mill with its roof lights to give an even illumination

That industrial scene, accompanied by many hundreds of smaller factories and workshops, occupied increasingly the land around the old town centre. Inevitably that town centre itself went through a transformation as complete as that of its surroundings.

The restored St Paul's House

The Corn Exchange a huge elliptical building with a magnificent dome.

New streets – like Albion Street, Commercial Street and Bond Street – had been added to the immediate west of the medieval core in the 18th and early 19th centuries. Now they and the streets leading towards the station became the commercial centre. Banks, one of the first of which in Leeds was Beckett's Bank (now incorporated into the National Westminster) were founded and in due course amalgamated with national banks. The Bank of England and the Midland Bank opened on suitably noticeable corner sites. The Leeds Club was founded in 1846 and placed in Albion Street behind a facade much altered later. Offices, insurance companies, building societies lined the main streets, substantial, expensive and apparently permanent, like the Yorkshire Bank of 1894. The Victorian town centre began to take shape.

And of course there were major new buildings standing in their own right. The Infirmary which had been behind the coloured Cloth Hall was demolished and a new one built, to designs by Gilbert Scott, in 1868 – the start of a major complex of medical buildings that now forms the Leeds General Infirmary. For those wanting some relief from it the Victoria Hotel was built at the same time (1867) and is still architecturally one of the finest pubs in Leeds. Still more outstanding were two astonishingly original public buildings – the Corn Exchange of 1861 and the Civic Institute (originally the Mechanics Institute) of 1865. The Corn Exchange, now cleaned, is a tough forbidding pile with diamond-rusticated masonry round the sides, a huge elliptical building with a dome that must have been a challenge to fit on the top, and a shaft of light from the part that is glazed. Everthing is curved – porch, ribs and steps. A gallery runs round the inside and from it you look down on the desks of the merchants. The Mechanics' Institute was an exercise in the style of the French Second Empire.

Both these buildings were designed by an architect who came into prominence as a result of a competition which was to provide Leeds with its most glorious building and a great civic headache.

Corn Exchange

Leeds Town Hall

Civic Pride

The story of the building of Leeds Town Hall is one of the sagas of Victorian England. It symbolised everything that Leeds stood for or felt guilty about. As its most enthusiastic advocate, Dr Heaton, said in a speech to the Philosophical and Literary Society in 1854, the Town Hall then being built would show that *"in the ardour of mercantile pursuits the inhabitants of Leeds have not omitted to cultivate the perception of the beautiful and a taste for the fine arts"*.

The competition for the design of the building was won in 1853 by a young architect from Hull, Cuthbert Brodrick, whose life story must be one of the few really satisfactory ones in the history of architecture. He had travelled extensively in France in 1844-5 and acquired a love for its classical architecture. He was only 29 when he won the competition for the Town Hall. He designed a relatively small number of buildings, all very significant ones, then retired before he was 50 to the south of France and lived happily ever after. As for Leeds, construction problems were constant and included the bankruptcy of the builder before the Town Hall was finished.

But that did not detract from the vigour of the design or the originality of its concept. Paid for out of the rates, it was planned to include law courts, a council chamber, a public hall, a suite of ceremonial entertaining-rooms and municipal offices. With the building of the Civic Hall in 1933 some of those functions moved away and it became essentially a public hall and law courts.

It is classical in style but baroque in imaginative power and drama. It stands squarely at the top of a huge flight of steps (altered from their original shape) on a mound made specially for the purpose. The whole facade is made of giant columns and all the sides reflect that pattern. The central portico has ten huge Corinthian columns. Then there is an immense frieze and rising above it all the central tower, 225 feet high, which was not there in the original design – a worthwhile but costly afterthought.

The Victoria Hall rises to 92 feet inside the parallelogram of surrounding rooms and corridors and the enclosing colonnades. The carving of the tympanum over the front entrance represents Leeds encouraging the Arts and Sciences. The Portland stone lions on either side, modelled at London Zoo, contrast with the sandstone of the building itself.

Until the Town Hall was cleaned recently some people thought it was built of solid coal; a hundred years of town smoke had covered the sandstone with a black velvet skin. It looked monstrous and awe-inspiring and was thought by many people best that way. But the cleaning revealed its wealth of carving and vigorous detail.

For Brodrick let himself go with a wealth of detail, not only outside but especially in the Victoria Hall – composite Corinthian columns and pilasters with the Leeds owl and the fleece designed into the capitals, ten cut-glass chandeliers of his design (replaced in 1878 and again in the 1930's), a stunning organ case in the apse of the hall and mottoes everywhere – *"Weave Truth with Trust"*, *"Honesty is the Best Policy"*, *"Good Will towards Men"*, and just *"Forward"*. It was, in the words of the chorus at the foundation ceremony, *"a trophy to Freedom – to Peace, and to Trade"*.

The foundation stone was laid with some pomp in 1853. But the pomp was nothing compared to that of the celebrations when it was opened by Queen Victoria, accompanied by Prince Albert, on 7 September 1858. She arrived the previous day at the Central Station,

From wherever you view it Leeds Town Hall with its splendid dome dominates Leeds. This vantage point is from St Paul's House.

A thoroughly majestic building with its dome, pillars and lions, the Town Hall adds a special attraction to the view from Park Square which is laid out to resemble the London squares

stayed with the Mayor, Peter Fairbairn, at his home, Woodsley House. On the day itself she proceeded down Woodhouse lane to the centre and along to the top of East Parade where a huge arch had been constructed so that the full glory of the Town Hall would break upon her at once.

The celebrations were tremendous. The opening was timed to coincide with an exhibition of local manufactures and a musical festival, which opened with Mendelson's *Elijah* and closed with Handel's *Messiah*. Police were reinforced from the West Riding, Bradford, London and Birmingham. Troops were everywhere in splendid regalia. The Queen inspected 32,110 children on Woodhouse Moor. The excitement grew by the hour. A chemist in Park Lane even perfumed the air outside his shop.

For many years the interior of the Town Hall was misleading. The original decorations, columns of marbled *rosso antico* with gilt bronze capitals and bases, podiums painted to seem inlaid with precious marbles, pale green spaces between the columns, with stained glass in the clerestory windows as well as the mottoes everywhere, were replaced in the late 1940's with pale wedding-cake colours. The immense organ, filling the apse, was almost apologetic.

Redecoration is now restoring its character. But whatever happened nothing could quite overcome the robustness and almost vulgar splendour of the Victoria Hall. The building had cost three times the architect's original estimate and was worth every penny.

Victoria Hall

Housing the workers

And yet, surrounding all this splendour and opulence, was a growing city distinguished by some of the worst housing that any industrial city produced. The Leeds back-to-back houses have become a byword for cheap and substandard housing of the 19th century.

The back-to-back house seems to have been a peculiarity of the North of England. But whereas in some towns a back-to-back means two rows of houses with a narrow alley between, the back-to-back in Leeds is literally so. The wall dividing the houses is immediately under the ridge of the roof of an apparently single block. That block has a house on one side and one on the other. Each house has therefore no back and no sides; it is enclosed on all sides but the front. There is a door (the only one into the house) and a few windows, rather small, to give light to the rooms. Because there is no back door or back yard, the washing is hung across the street. And because there is no place for a privy, before the days of internal water closets, there was a group of privies at the end of the block.

How did this happen? With the huge growth of the town in the first forty years of the 19th century workers poured into Leeds, leaving the countryside or migrating from Ireland and other countries. The back-to-back house was simply the answer to the need for cheap housing. Thirty thousand of them were built by 1844, another twenty-eight thousand between then and 1874, another twelve thousand by 1909. Despite the bye-laws passed under the Public Health Act, Leeds went on building them well into the twentieth century. The last one was put up in 1937.

The earliest probably happened more or less accidentally, as houses were jammed up against each other in some of the yards and closes of the old town. it was a different matter to design them from scratch.

The first layout of that type was just east of Vicar Lane, a development that included back-to-backs and cellar dwellings. Then another group was put up near the river. At the turn of the century they spread to the northeast and south of the river. What dictated their layout was simply the policy of getting as many houses as possible on to the plot of land available. Since the plots available were fields of irregular shapes, bought from different owners and butting on to each other at odd

Nineteenth century living conditions in the centre of Leeds: this is Lambert's Yard in Lower Briggate.

angles: and since the simplest way to build as many houses as possible was to lay them out in parallel rows down the longest dimension of the field, it followed there would be no discernible urban layout, merely a collection of rows, meeting at strange angles, with blank walls and sudden changes in level. It seems extraordinary that no one should have cared about the total formal chaos as well as the living conditions that such housing promoted. As D H Lawrence wrote later *"our towns are false towns - every street a blow, every corner a stab"*.

The worst of the back-to-backs – one up and one down, cottages about 15 feet square – were the earliest ones, none of which remain. After 1866 local bye-laws made it obligatory to leave more room between the rows and to build them in blocks of no more than eight – four front and four back, so that privies could be built in yards between each block. Later ones were larger, with more and bigger rooms; and some had small gardens on each side, and could be arranged in almost picturesque groups. They are regarded by many people with affection and nostalgia.

The building of the back-to-backs was a constant subject of dispute. Robert Baker, writing about them at the time of the governmental enquiry into the Sanitary Conditions of the Labouring Classes, commented that "To build the largest number of cottages in the smallest available space seems to have been the original view of the speculators". What was obvious was not only that they were crowded together but that the houses were overcrowded themselves and were a source of ill health. Reports proved that the incidence of cholera and other contagious diseases and the rate of death were

Terraces of back-to-backs cluster round the grim walls of Armley Gaol. Above, a typical scene in a red-brick Leeds terrace.

dramatically worst in the areas of worst housing. It was partly the back-to-backs that inspired the characteristics of today's health legislation. They were, after all, short of light and air; what the new bye-laws demanded (and still do) was big enough windows and through ventilation.

In 1871 on the recommendation of the medical officer 293 houses were pulled down in Wellington Yard. The yard had featured in every epidemic since 1832. In it was an open midden 21' long, 5'10" wide and 6' deep; a drunken man fell in one night and was suffocated. In the same year the Corporation decided to clear some of the becks leading into the Aire, which was becoming more and more disgusting. Out of one they took the carcases of 7 cats, 11 rats, 17 dogs and 6 pigs. The new medical officer reported in 1891 about the Marsh Lane-Quarry Hill area that there were 7,700 people in back-to-backs around tiny courts with an average density of 200 to the acre, with parts at densities of 274 and 314. It was not surprising that the typhoid outbreak of 1889 hit such areas particularly hard.

The back-to-backs were deposited like red brick pebbles by a tide washing right up into the valleys and leaving behind packed houses, filling every crevice, jammed into every nook, settling down around every major building and every eminence of land. Though some on hilltops and slopes could look more attractive than others, most were visibly the same. There were so many that when the developers had exhausted every variation on a name – Harold Avenue, Harold Grove, Harold Mount, Harold View, Harold Walk – they simply named the streets by numbers. A well known group which was near Armley Gaol and has since been demolished, numbered 1st to 18th Avenue.

And if that was not enough, over everywhere hung the great pall of smoke from the factories, the dye-houses, the workshops and above all the domestic chimneys. The colour of the buildings that have not yet been cleaned gives some idea of what must have been the colour inside people's lungs.

It inspired William Osburn's celebrated lines, read in 1857 to members of the Leeds Philosophical and Literary Society:

"The Aire below is doubly dyed and damned;
The Air above with lurid smoke is crammed;
The One flows steaming foul as Charon's Styx,
Its poisonous vapours in the other mix.
These sable twins the murky town invest –
By them the skin's begrimed, the lungs oppressed.
How dear the penalty thus paid for wealth;
Obtained through wasted life and broken health".

Suburban style

But that impression of inadequacy and gloom is only one face of the Leeds that took shape in the 19th century. Of course there were the gloomier parts – like Armley Gaol, built in 1847 and enlarged and made fiercer and more fortified ten years later. But for the most part as the century wore on Leeds must have been a rattling, noisy, friendly vivid place. Even in the back-to-backs, Leeds does not give the impression of disaster and misery that you get from the accounts of some of the other northern cities. But what must have been tremendous was the life of the spreading suburbs.

As the low cost housing filled up the gaps among the factories and moved in to the areas that had once been smart close to the town centre, the middle classes, the professional people and the business-men, moved further afield. The richer people, following the example of the previous generation, built villas and houses, often in exotic styles – Gothic fantasies like Meanwood Towers by the younger Pugin in 1867, or Spenfield designed by George Corson in 1876, filled with marble columns and stained glass, brass and ornate plasterwork.

But the suburbs also contained the homes of the less opulent middle classes. For them the crucial event was the setting up of the tramways in 1871.

The trams have now gone from the streets, to the regret of some but possibly the improvement of the general environment. The Tramway Museum Society retains some of them. The earliest were pulled by horses, then driven by steam, but it was the electric trams that brought the suburbs within daily reach of so many families and made it possible for people without transport of their own to live more than a walk from their work. From Headingley and Harehills, from Roundhay and Chapel Allerton, men set off to the nearest tram stop in the morning, gradually building up a society of the tramstop.

The trams had a character of their own; some seemed grudging, badtempered and unwilling; some were quick off the mark, smooth and jolly; all had something to say about community and the visible links between people. For those who lived in the city centre and could not get to a place as far away as Roundhay Park when it was taken over by the Corporation and opened as a

Leeds was one of the tramway pioneers with the first lines opening in 1871 and electric trams coming into service in the 1890s. The top picture shows Briggate with its horse trams and, below Lower Briggate when the electric tramcars had taken over.

public park in 1872, a special tram service was laid on.

It is difficult to exaggerate the importance of trams in making possible and desirable the extension of cities and the development of suburbs. It became possible to live away from soot and noise and crowded housing, but near enough for a daily journey of half an hour or less.

Those first tram lines in Leeds opened in 1871, following fast on the Tramways Act of 1870. The fleets of horse–trams, with their drivers and "guards", were replaced by electric trams in the 1890's. Then the Corporation extended the electric system to the whole city in 1896, giving Leeds the first municipally owned and operated electric tramway in the country.

The first electrified line ran from Kirkstall to Roundhay and was rapidly followed by others in an increasingly complex network of tracks. How colourful and vigorous they looked, with contrasting strong colours and adverisements all over them, at first with open tops, then with canvas screens, then enclosed. They were at their best in what has come to be known as the Golden Age of Tramways, from the turn of the century until the middle of the twenties. By then in Leeds there were goods lines and the famous Middleton Light Railway on its own reservation, opened in 1925 to provide a link to a major council housing development.

And it was possible, with a few changes, to get from the centre of Leeds to the centre of Bradford. Between 1900 and 1911 routes were opened to Morley, Stanningley, Pudsey, Horsforth, Guiseley, Rothwell and Wakefield. More amazing still, you could go by tram from Leeds to Liverpool with a gap of only eight miles from Hebden Bridge to Summit.

The trams were abandoned in 1954, but their effect upon the city was permanent.

Because so many people of moderate or substantial

The carved staircase of Spenfield, a mansion designed by George Corson in 1876

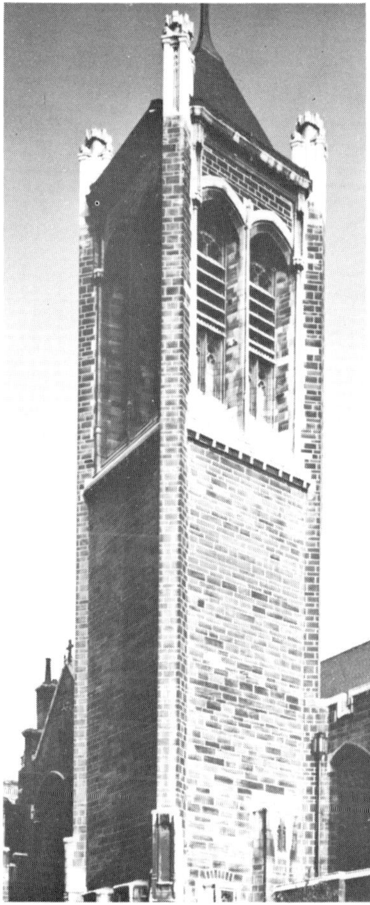

The churches of Leeds in Victorian times were impressive. An example of their style is St Chad's Far Headingley, seen left in an exterior and interior view. St Anne's cathedral, below replaced the original building, erected in 1838.

means could travel by public transport to the suburbs, the suburbs took on a new character and remain some of the most colourful and attractive areas in Leeds today – houses of dark stone, with handsome porches, or fantastic gables and roofs with cast-iron cresting along the ridge, stone mullioned windows, steps, gates and gateposts with carved tops and huge iron hinges. Near Roundhay Park they were especially fanciful. But then so they were on the slopes above Kirkstall Abbey, in Gledhow Valley and elsewhere. All such houses had one or more servants, as most middle class families had until the Great War. But the houses varied greatly in size and form. There were terraces, single houses, villas and ornamental cottages. And everywhere big trees, thick shrubberies close to the house and plants inside as well as out.

In those suburbs were built impressive churches, like the Church of St Chad at Far Headingley , designed by Lord Grimthorpe (one of the Becketts) in 1868. Or there was St Aidan's, Roundhay Road. That was suburban but is now effectively a major city centre edifice. Just as interesting and architecturally more original was the new Catholic cathedral. The church of 1838 became a cathedral in 1878 when the new Catholic diocese was established. But it was in the way of the road improvements at the end of the century. The new St Anne's by J H Eastwood was opened a little up Cookridge Street in 1902.

More evocative was the Woodhouse Cemetery, with elaborate monuments and huge gates, on the edge of the Moor which was the centre of funfairs and days out, with its statues of Queen Victoria and also Wellington and Peel who had been moved there when they were kicked out of the square in front of the Town Hall. It was a substantial, prosperous and stable world, with all the excitement and gaiety of the society that was destroyed by the Great War.

The old St Anne's Cathedral

City Centre

City Markets

The town centre was now the centre of what had become a city in 1893. What fun it must have been, how colourful and how varied. For the more serious there was the Public Library, part of the Municipal Buldings of 1884, with its extraordinary staircase, by George Corson, the same architect as Spenfield – a fantasy of arches and landings and wrought iron railings, with Byzantine decoration and marvellous coloured tiles – an aesthetic pleasure to take a book out of it.

Not far away, making a new centre for the city, was the opened up City Square. In the 1880's the old Coloured Cloth Hall had been replaced by a new General Post Office. The present building went up in 1896. In 1891 the adjoining Quebec estate was purchased by the Corporation so as to make a dignified open space. The layout has been modified since it was designed in 1896, but the main features of it are still there. They include the equestrian statue of the Black Prince (they had to have an equestian statue if the place were to rival the towns of Italy, even if the relevance of the Black Prince to Leeds was tenuous) and four pairs of ladies representing Morn and Eve holding electric

County Arcade

Among the glories of Leeds are its theatres with their reminders of a time when no expense was spared to turn theatres into palaces of fantasy. On the left, the elaborate moulding on the ceiling of the Grand Theatre, and below, the period charm of the City Varieties which television has brought to an appreciative audience of millions.

Leeds City Market, renovated after being gutted in the disastrous fire.

globes. Statues of Dean Hook and Joseph Priestley were added later, politely facing away. For a few years Alderman T W Harding, who had initiated the project, paid for a uniformed attendant to look after the square and the statues and stop people striking matches on the ladies' bottoms. So popular did the city square nudes become that when in 1961 they were removed for the sake of remodelling the square, public protests led to their replacement a year later.

But really the town centre was a shopping centre. At the other end from City Square were the City Markets, built in 1857 but with an exterior rebuilt by the brothers Leeming in 1904. If you couldn't find what you wanted there you could walk down the Arcades, one of the specialities of Leeds, crossing the main streets, threading through the blocks, croosing them at right angles, Thorntons of 1878 or the County of 1898, with cast iron roofs and tiled decoration and little men coming out from a clock to announce the hour.

At the end of the day you could go to the Grand Theatre, built in 1878, the biggest of the provincial theatres, gloriously decorated (again by George Corson) with plaster and gilded papier-mache, dripping with luxury and boastfulness. Or you could go to the smaller and older City Varieties, the home of the music hall, now creating nostalgia for the good old days. And you could drop in to a public house like Whitelocks, an ancient tavern in one of the oldest of the yards opening on Briggate, still a complete Edwardian interior. You can still imagine it all because the essence of it is still there.

Staircase, City Library

Marks and Spencer's Bazaar

A new society

In 1881 the Tsar of Russia, Alexander II, was assassinated. The outrage led to fierce disorders and a series of pogroms. Anti-Jewish feeling, never far from the surface, made the Jews scapegoats. Large numbers were expelled from Russia and Eastern Europe. It was a disaster; but for Leeds it was an unexpected piece of luck.

Many of the Jews, sailing from Northern Europe, landed at Hull and worked their way across northern England, on their way, it is said, to Liverpool, the Atlantic and the land of milk and honey at the other side of it. On the way they stopped at Leeds and many of them went no further. For they discovered that they could fill a gap at a crucial moment in the development of the Leeds manufacturing industry. By the end of Queen Victoria's reign 15,000 Jews had settled in Leeds.

Their arrival can be taken as signalling the start of the modern era in Leeds. It was not only that the Jews set up small shops and workshops to supplement the output of the clothing factories and warehouses. Their skills, as tailors and clothiers, were precisely those needed by a city in which the old Cloth Halls and the merchants had less of a role to play and which had moved into the field of ready-made clothing and the manufacture of cheap cloths.

The first firm to exploit their skills was Barran's, whose founder had built the great warehouse in Park Square in 1878. Barran's were pioneers. By the end of the century, Leeds had huge factories, using mechanical cutting knives and sewing machines, making garments and selling them at the rate of about five million a year.

Within an astonishingly short time of arriving the Jewish community had become organised. The inscription on a building in Regent Street suggests that they were able to form unions almost on arrival. They took only a little longer to organise religiously. The Great Synagogue was built in Belgrave Street. Later came the new Great Synagogue in Chapeltown Road.

Other synagogues and their siting reflected the movement of the Jewish community further out as their fortunes improved. From the little shops in North Street they moved northwards, to areas like Chapel Allerton, Moortown and Alwoodley. As they moved out, coloured people later took their place – just as they had

A new and significant shape on the Leeds skyline. This is the Great Synagogue in Chapeltown Road.

themselves to some extent taken the place of the Irish immigrants who had arrived some fifty years before.

Those changes are symptomatic of far-reaching changes which were happening in the shape of Leeds industries at the end of the 19th century and the early years of the twentieth. Two were especially significant.

The first was the decision of Joseph Hepworth and Sons (taken about 1883) not only to manufacture garments but to sell them in their own retail shops.

The second, elaborating upon Barran's example, was the development of bespoke made-to-measure clothing in wholesale quantities. It was Montague Burton who innovated this – a piece of simple brilliance (like all strokes of genius) when he appreciated that most people have physical similarities and that it must be possible to apply mass production methods to individual tailoring by the use of standard ranges of dimensions – and thus provide a cheap tailor-made suit for the working man virtually off the peg. By 1921 Burton's Hudson Road Mills were the biggest of their kind in the country.

The variety of Leeds industry continued – heavy engineering (a vast number of locomotives has been exported from Leeds in the last 150 years; the copper works was founded in 1879), street lanterns (first exhibited by their inventor, George Bray, outside the Town Hall in 1879), lawnmowers, sausage chopping machines, armaments (sold to all sides), matches, candles, hats and caps, shoes and boots (especially heavy ones), footballs (one firm used to buy 500 hides at a time for making them) and, of course, second-hand clothing. Today half the working population of the city is employed in manufacturing industry. This broad base and variety is said to have kept Leeds stable and prosperous.

Against that background of manufacturing industry, studies in science and technology, and then in humanities, were increasingly developed.

In 1874 had been founded the Yorkshire College of Science. It was the nucleus of a university. The Clothworkers Court (and the Great Hall) was built in 1877. To the College was added the School of Medicine, which had been founded in 1831, but became the Faculty of Medicine in 1884. The whole college was then incorporated into the Victoria University, an imaginative experiment to form a regional university out of the Yorkshire College, Owen's College in Manchester and University College in Liverpool, which like most imaginative ideas was found to be unworkable. Leeds University received its Charter and its independence in 1904.

From that moment the University grew. There were setbacks during the Great War and the Depression; but from the thirties the University expanded and took on a new shape. Although the Parkinson Building was only completed after the Second World War, it was essentially a pre-war concept – to give the Unversity an imposing entrance. It rested on a basic misconception – that there was anywhere outside it from which you could appreciate how symmetrical and magnificent the building was – but it gave a centre and a presence to an important new component in the city.

That plan was radically transformed after the Second World War. Leeds University had the first methodical plan for systematic growth in numbers and facilities. The long glass and concrete buildings, which include what is said to be the longest straight corridor in Europe, embody a plan for continuous development enclosing spaces which have been carved out of the demolition of substandard housing and the formation of a precinct for academic work.

In the arts, in music and in education, Leeds became much more than a manufacturing town.

In 1907 the Corporation purchased the richly landscaped Beckett Park and its house Kirkstall Grange, and built the City of Leeds College of Education. The Carnegie College of Physical Education was built on the

Leeds University has grown organically and is a mixture of styles, with the elegant Great Hall, and right the modern style of the newer additions.

same site in 1933. They were not alone. The College of Technology developed from the Mechanics' Institute founded in the 1820's, the College of Commerce from evening classes started in 1898; the College of Art was founded in 1846 and by the 1960's had become one of the most dynamic and provocative art institutions in the country. In 1970 those three were merged with the Yorkshire College of Education and Home Economics to form Leeds Polytechnic. In 1976 the whole lot were amalgamated to form the new Polytechnic – one of the largest and most comprehensive educational institutions in the country.

Growth of a similar kind happened also in the medical field. The Infirmary, which had moved to its site in Great George Street in 1868, was enlarged by the Brotherton Wing. Even more massive was the growth of St. James's Hospital. That hospital received its name in 1927; its origin – what is now the northern section – was the old Union Workhouse, started in 1861. St James's Hospital is now the biggest general hospital in the United Kingdom.

The size of institutions may not be very significant in itself. But here it reflects a basic general change of our day, and one which Leeds happens vividly to symbolise.

Take the clothing industry. It is essential to an understanding of that – as of most modern industry and the development of all modern towns since the Industrial Revolution – that the market which makes such development possible is the mass market, not the special prestige one. That only requires small traders and workshops; it is at the moment that the majority of people – that is, the working man – can afford to go

The impressive Civic Institute, at the start of the cultural and educational enclave in Cookridge Street.

shopping, that the modern town centre and modern industry takes off.

In 1884 Michael Marks, a Polish Jewish immigrant, set up his famous Penny Bazaar in Leeds market. His son Simon, who took over the business in 1909, recognised the possibilities of selling quality goods of many kinds, and built up a chain of stores, Marks and Spencer, which have had a profound effect on almost all town centres in Great Britain as well as in Leeds itself. The multiple store with its increasingly sophisticated methods of

The Headrow, which became the heart of Leeds, pictured before its rebuilding.

selling and the need for large floor spaces, had become a feature of all town centres.
The town centre, in other words, became a commercial centre – for shopping and offices; and that is one of the crucial phenomena of our day. Briggate, the street on which the whole commerce of Leeds was originally based, was gradually lined with chain stores. The yards became back-yards. The residents moved out – and then came back in to do their shopping. Then the place went through another major change. The symbol of the whole process is the Headrow.

Until 1924 the Headrow was merely a lane (or "row") at the top (the "head") of the 80 acres that was Leeds before the Industrial Revolution set it spreading. In 1924 the Corporation decided that it was necessary to transform it, to link up Eastgate and Westgate and provide not only a wider road but a new east-west route through the city to relieve the already congested centre around Boar Lane and City Square. The head row was in any case by now in the very heart of the city.

What the building of the Headrow did was effectively to turn Leeds round again. The original grain of the city ran North to South, with Briggate as the spine of the whole thing. The Industrial Revolution – and Gott's Mill – had turned it back to front; now the Shopping Revolution turned it round on its side – at right angles. For the new city centre ran east to west, with the Headrow as the posh shopping street, Eastgate and Westgate extending it.

The Headrow was designed by an eminent architect, Sir Reginald Blomfield. No one could pretend that architecturally it was likely to send the spirits soaring; but it opened the way to major stores like Lewis's who built in a style more or less in keeping with Sir Reginald's.

It was the new grand city street, At one end, at the west, was the Town Hall. And to the east (typical of this unpredictable city) they built, not another public building, a monument or a memorial, but the biggest block of council flats in Europe – Quarry Hill.

Beckett Park

Leeds Polytechnic

Recasting the City

It was unusual enough to make Council housing the main feature of a civic development, especially as it took the place of some unusually bad slums which at the beginning of the century had been designated as the Quarry Hill Unhealthy Area. It was even more unusual to build a huge scheme of a wholly experimental and revolutionary nature, which became a visiting place for town planners and housing managers from all over the world. The driving force behind it was the Vicar of Holbeck, the Rev. Charles Jenkinson, a Christian Socialist who became a councillor when Labour came to power in 1933.

Quarry Hill was designed and built between 1934 and 1940, inspired by housing estates in Vienna and Berlin in the twenties and thirties. It had a site of 26 acres; and consisted of 938 flats, housing over 3,000 people.

Its form was revolutionary. It was part of the brief that not more than one-fifth of the site should be built on; the rest was to be open space, for playing and gardens, for fresh air and relaxation. (In fact only 18% was built on). It had a shopping centre, playgrounds (completed after the war), a laundry, a day nursery; it should have had a social centre and a sports area, which were never completed.

Just as unusual, it was constructed in a new building system, the Mopin system, using light steel frames and concrete facing slabs; and it employed, for the first time in this country, the Garchcy system of refuse disposal, with refuse chutes from the kitchen of each flat through which all the refuse was dropped and sucked to a central incinerator plant which served as a heating plant for the central laundry.

There were lifts to all floors. The buildings varied in height from four storeys at the east end to eight down the slope at Eastgate, where the huge parabolic arch of the entrance became one of the features of the Leeds scene.

The disadvantages of Quarry Hill were inherent in its innovatory nature. There were faults in its cladding, its structure became subject to damp and corrosion, technical problems led to escalating costs in repairs. With a characteristic failure of vision and will, the authority left out some of the crucial social buildings and allowed the landscape proposals to degenerate into waste. In 1978, less than 40 years after its construction,

The dramatic sweep of Quarry Hill Flats, vision-come-true of the Rev Charles Jenkinson

Quarry Hill was demolished.

Quarry Hill was only the culmination of a series of projects of council housing in which Leeds Corporation was a leading exponent between the wars, following the Housing and Town Planning Act of 1919. One of the earliest was the Middleton scheme, two storey cottage-type houses formally laid out. Nearby was Belle Isle. Others included the scheme at Gipton and parts of the development at Seacroft. Leeds, with its frightening back-log of substandard housing from the 19th century, became one of the pioneers of council housing and has tried out almost every type that can be seen in this country.

Surprisingly, Leeds was not seriously bombed during

the Second World War. Partly because of that, it did not start to redevelop itself seriously until much later than other cities. That enabled Leeds to avoid some of the obvious mistakes made in the course of hurried rebuilding in other places. But it also meant that when redevelopment did start, in the late fifties, it was a colossal explosion – in effect, nothing less than the rebuilding of the city.

It coincided, and was profoundly influenced by, the presence in Leeds during the sixties of an unusually able group of civic leaders, many of whom became national figures – a rare partnership of far-sighted and determined councillors and exceptionally able officers. Together they set about achieving what a leading officer described as the resurgence of the city.

Two things in particular made this possible. The first was the housing need. It was estimated in 1948 that Leeds still possessed, out of a total of 154,000 houses, 90,000 which were substandard and required demolition (among them about 56,000 back-to-back houses); in addition there was the general postwar housing shortage. The second was the need to do something about the traffic.

The two needs were neatly matched. For the worst unfit housing crammed in during the Industrial Revolution, was in the place where new roads were wanted – the twilight inner ring immediately surrounding the central area.

The coincidence of the two needs geographically meant that almost the whole of that inner ring of the city could be rebuilt, with new housing, new commercial areas, open space and new roads, replacing the areas of industrial housing and semi-derelict small works. At the same time, so as to absorb the industries and people from the centre, the city could spread at the edges and form new comprehensive areas on the perimeter.

The pattern of location of industry was wholly changed. In the previous few decades the main industrial areas had become concentrated mainly in three areas; heavy engineering around the river, from Kirkstall in the west to Stourton in the east, with the new power station there as well; tanneries and wholesale clothing in the Meanwood Valley; light engineering as well as heavy engineering and textile mills across the river in Hunslet and Holbeck, Armley and Wortley. Now industry moved out from the old industrial heart by the river to new areas on the outer ring or the radials.

Of the 270,000 people employed in Leeds, about 140,00 were in manufacturing industry. They were now concentrated in industrial areas, related, no longer to the railway and its goods yards, but to the new urban motorways, the M1 and the M62, with access by them to the north and south, the east and west across the Pennines.

If industry moved out – to be nearer the new communications – housing now began to move back in and that constituted another basic reversal in Leeds. To pursue the image used earlier, the Industrial Revolution had turned the city back to front; the station turned it upside down; the Headrow turned it on its side; the new motorway system finally turned it inside out.

All those changes make Leeds virtually a prototype of the modern city – socially as well as geographically. The modern city has to be the city of the common man. Its

Potternewton Court, one of the newer housing developments

prestige buildings are not churches and monuments; they are buildings for the extension of the personalities, and satisfaction of the needs of everyman. More than anything else, the great monuments of modern environmental design – and the chief users of urban land – are houses.

After Quarry Hill, in the same end of the city, the Corporation created the Saxton Gardens scheme of 450 flats, then Ebor Gardens with 1151 dwellings. But the biggest scheme is Seacroft, which houses between 80,000 and 85,000 people. Some of this answered the demands created by slum clearance, at the rate of between 1,500 and 2,000 houses a year. Other schemes reflected general housing demand.

By the time of local government reorganisation there were about 168,000 houses in Leeds, over 70,000 of them owned by the Corporation. Some substantial private projects of private housing, as dull, pretentious and standard as anywhere else, have been erected. But the Council's work still dominated the scene. For in the postwar years the Council deliberately made an onslaught on housing demand, and built massive schemes, many of them multi-storey.

The concentration on housing, sometimes at the expense of other related facilities, meant that the most urgent housing needs were met. Now the policy is towards more varied kinds of environment, an abandonment of the multi-storey blocks, and an emphasis on the environment as a whole – not only houses, but the spaces around them, the landscape, the local shops, the social building. The Little London development reveals clearly the change of policy from high building to

Trees and paved courtyards are features of the development in Town Street, Chapel Allerton.

two-storey terraced housing. To the north the biggest and most comprehensive project is the Holt Park development, effectively a New Town. And there are small schemes like Potternewton Court, and Town Street, Chapel Allerton, beautifully laid out around a pedestrian walk.

The later projects represent an attempt to create a new intermingled, comprehensive urban form, with housing, schools, shopping centres and open spaces, forming a new continuous landscape of work and play and living – the scattering of the park throughout the town – a total environment that may one day incorporate a revivified canal and River Aire, long despoiled by industry and neglected as a potentially valuable leisure facility.

It is a major change. Having been for centuries a city founded on the waterways, Leeds with dramatic suddenness has become the city at the crossroads of the motorways. Access to the south is provided by the M1. Access eastwards to Hull and westwards to Liverpool, achieving at last a successful crossing of the Pennines, is by the M62. Leeds, in the middle of the network, seems a logical place for London businesses to establish their branches; a centre for insurance and finance, a major service and distribution point.

And that means changes in the city centre, the commercial, office and shopping centre, which has been undergoing a transformation as great as in the 19th century. There are new buildings, new groups and comprehensive schemes, new offices. Many of them are as ill-designed and uninteresting as those of every other postwar city. What makes the centre of Leeds a landmark today is the reorganisation of its streets and of its traffic.

In the early sixties, Leeds was one of the cities examined in the Buchanan Report on *Traffic in Towns.* It had already begun its own traffic planning, exploring a new concept. In partnership with the Ministry of Transport and the Ministry of Housing and Local

City of motorways including the Inner Ring Road.

Government from 1965 the Council carried out a major study and began a massive programme of work in pursuit of what was called *The Leeds Approach.*

The Inner Ring Road, cutting below the level of most of the existing streets and circling the northern part of the central area to take cross-town traffic and guide it away from the streets in the city centre, is one component. It links to existing and new radial roads, but also to the motorways. On that Inner Ring Road is the first of what was planned as a series of multi-storey car parks. And that indicates the nature of this plan for a modern city.

For the reorganisation of the city centre is devised, not to cater for all the motorcars which are forecast, nor for their exclusion, if that were possible. It is based upon a simple and basic idea – that the key to an integrated transport system is parking.

What, after all, ultimately determines the crowdedness and bustle of a city centre is not how many cars get through, but what the people do when they get out of their cars, and what they do with the cars when they leave them. In every city, a large number leave their cars alone, occupying a space for a day while they themselves stay in an office; for them it is better to leave the cars outside the city centre – in one of the car parks. Others must bring them in; traders and shopkeepers must have access. Others again are going shopping.

The essence of the Leeds Approach was to give priority of access to private cars used for business and shopping and set a limit to private car commuting. The key to that was to provide parking in the central area for only 20% of the possible demand from commuters. But that entailed developing an efficient system of public transport.

The future city centre depends no doubt upon integrated policies in public transport, parking, traffic management and planning generally. There is less faith around now in what planners propose and less confidence that plans will ever be carried through to completion.

Quarry Hill

Relief in precinct

On foot again

The scheme for Leeds will probably never be complete. But it has made possible an essential part of the plan – an imaginative and exciting redirection of the central streets – which puts Leeds in the forefront of planning experiments. For the new roads and the parking policies have made it possible to transform some of the Victorian streets in the city centre into an extensive pedestrian area – the largest in the country.

And what a revelation it is. Start at the eastern end, where it crosses Briggate, the spine of the original town, and links to the Arcades, seeming to extend them to the full, stretch their possibilities and bring them all together. Walk along, as an ever-increasing number of shoppers and town-walkers do, along the paved walks that were once streets, with varied paving and setts, trees and sculptures; and suddenly the old streets are a revelation. They invite you to raise your eyes and look at the buildings and see for the first time what you had never noticed before.

The town – and its buildings – come to life, and, astonishingly, you are in the midst, no longer of drab Victorian gloom, but of Victorian vulgarity and fun. Go

Lands Lane pedestrian precinct

A rooftop view of Leeds reveals the astounding range of architecture, from contemporary to 18th century.

to the west end of it, into the office area first developed in the early 19th century, to Bond Court, to see where the footstreets relate to the traffic streets, where cars poke their noses mildly through a facade, and what the scale is of a modern town centre – the scale of the courts that take the place of the old smaller courts of the early industrial era.

For this is the heart, not just of the city, but of the matter. Can a modern city, with its crowds, its assembly of consumer goods, its commuters and its traffic, its cars and buses and other machines, still keep a human scale – one which we can recognise, where we can belong and have some dignity and self-respect?

The experiment with the footstreets of Leeds is an attempt to achieve that – to separate the functions, to cater for just enough machines, but ultimately to relate it all to Man – to put him back on his feet and give him freedom – to move around, to think, to see, to talk, to engage in the civic life which is the meaning of civilisation.

Meantime the reorganisation of local government if 1973 has made Leeds both larger and more powerful as well as possibly more uncertain of its future. With the division of planning powers so that transportation comes under the county authority centred in Wakefield, it is unlikely that the planned road system envisaged in the Leeds Approach will ever be completed. But public opinion has in any case changed, and the dimming of the image of the "Motorway City of the 70's" may not be regretted.

On the other hand Leeds is now bigger than ever, a Metropolitan District of over three quarters of a million people. It describes itself as the Capital of the Centre of Britain, with the size, importance and economic and social resources to take its place as a major European city. It may be, as its publicity says, on the threshold of a great surge forward. Some critics (and some economists) say not. It will, as ever, depend upon the conviction and determination of the people in authority and the people of the city who make it all work.

LEEDS CITY CENTRE

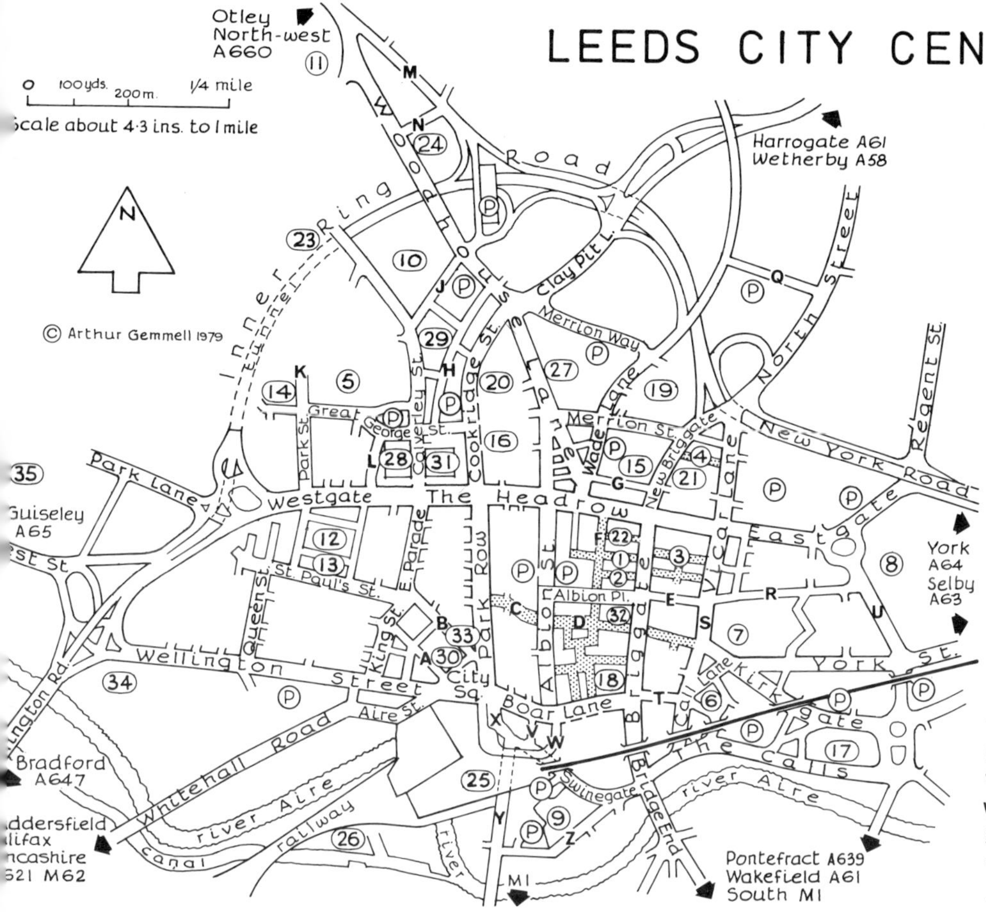

SYMBOLS

- pedestrian precinct
- (P) off-street car park

SECONDARY STREETS

A Quebec St.
B Infirmary St.
C Bond St.
D Commercial St.
E King Edward St.
F Lands Lane
G Mark Lane
H Portland Cres.
J Portland Way
K Thoresby Place
L Oxford Place
M Blenheim Walk
N Blackman Lane
Q Grafton St.
R George St.
S New Market St.
T Duncan St.
U St. Peter's St.
V Mill Hill
W New Station St.
X Bishopgate St.
Y Neville St.
Z Sovereign St.

FEATURES

1 Thornton's arcade
2 Queen's "
3 County "
4 Grand "
5 Infirmary
6 Corn Exchange
7 Kirkgate market
8 Quarry Hill
9 Queen's Hall
10 Polytechnic
11 University
12 Park Square
13 St. Paul's House
14 St. George's Church
15 St. John's "
16 St. Anne's "
17 Parish "
18 Trinity "
19 Former Synagogue
20 Civic Theatre — College of Music
21 Grand Theatre
22 City Varieties
23 Leeds Playhouse
24 BBC
25 Railway station
26 Canal
27 Merrion Centre
28 Town Hall
29 Civic Hall
30 Post Office
31 Library, Art Gall., Museum
32 Whitelock's
33 Yorkshire Bank
34 Yorkshire Post
35 Yorkshire T.V.

Index

Index

Index

Armley House